CELEBRATING THE 50TH ANNIVERSARY OF THE FIRST MOON LANDING

Every night while I was growing up, the brightly glowing Moon helped light the path to my dreams. I looked up at its cratered surface in wonder. I read science fiction books about living there. I did a school project on where the Moon may have come from. At the seaside I marvelled at the tides as the Moon magically pulled the water up and down.

But it was on a hot July night that my dreamy thoughts became real. The brave, skilled astronauts of Apollo 11 travelled to that distant place and stepped out onto its surface, their boots blazing a new trail in the ancient grey dust. Those footprints showed me that impossible things can happen.

It changed who I imagined I could be. That night, I decided to turn myself into an astronaut.

Years later, as I floated weightless in my spaceship, I peered through the window at that same Moon, so beautiful and alluring in the pitch black sky. I smiled, shook my head, and said a small inadequate thank-you to the Moon, and to everyone who had helped make my dreams come true.

Chris Hadfield

Chris Hadfield
Astronaut

The
Darkest Dark

To my children, Kyle, Evan and Kristin – together we find the way past our fears – C.H.

For Tristan and Chas, my favourite explorers – K.F.

For Tara, who lit the path – T.F. & E.F.

First published 2016 simultaneously in the UK by Macmillan Children's Books and in the US by Tundra Books
This edition published 2019 by Macmillan Children's Books
an imprint of Pan Macmillan
20 New Wharf Road, London N1 9RR
Associated companies throughout the world
www.panmacmillan.com

ISBN 978-1-5290-1361-0

Interior photo credits: page 44, all photos courtesy of Chris Hadfield; page 45,
all photos of Chris courtesy of NASA; photo of Chris and Albert courtesy of Terry Fan and Eric Fan.

1 3 5 7 9 8 6 4 2

A CIP catalogue record for this book is available from the British Library.

Printed in China

The Darkest Dark

Written by CHRIS HADFIELD and KATE FILLION
Illustrated by THE FAN BROTHERS

Macmillan Children's Books

Chris was an astronaut. An important and very busy astronaut.

When it was time to take a bath, he told his mother,
"I'd love to, but I'm saving the planet from aliens."

When it was time to get out of the bath and go to bed,
he told his father – politely, because astronauts are always polite –
"Sorry, no can do. I'm on my way to Mars."

An astronaut's work is never done,
so astronauts do not like to sleep.

But their parents do.

"You're a big boy now," said Chris's father.
"You have to sleep in your own bed."

And Chris tried, he really did,
but his room was dark. Very, very dark.

The kind of dark
that attracts the
worst sort of aliens.

But his parents meant it.

Chris. Was. Going. To. Sleep.
In. His. Own. Bed. *Tonight.*

His mum and dad checked under his bed and in the wardrobe,
and even in his underwear drawer. They declared the room
one hundred per cent alien-free.

They tucked Chris in.
They turned on the night-light.
They even gave him a special
bell to ring if he was nervous.

They took away the bell.

And then his father said something that worried Chris even more than the dark did. "One more peep, young man, and I'm afraid we'll all be too tired to go next door tomorrow."

But tomorrow would be a special day. A very special day. Chris *had* to go next door. His life pretty much depended on it.

So Chris stayed in his own bed. Without a peep. It took a long time to fall asleep, but when he did, he had his favourite dream . . .

He flew his spaceship all the way to the Moon.

The next day seemed to last forever. But finally, when the Moon was shining over the lake and the summer wind was ruffling the leaves of the trees, Chris ran next door.

The house was already full of people, all gathered
around the TV – the only TV on the whole island.

Chris found a spot where he could see through the crowd.
And what he saw was . . .

Astronauts. Real, live astronauts. On the actual, far-away Moon.
They were wearing puffy white suits and jumping for joy —
jumping so high, because there was so much less gravity there.

The grown-ups huddled around the TV were amazed. Their whole lives long, they'd never expected to see this sight. Even Chris (who had been to the Moon just the night before) was amazed. He'd never really noticed how *dark* it was there.

That night, Chris did a little experiment.
He turned off all the lights in his room,
even the night-light. It was still dark.
Very, *very* dark. There were still shadows
that looked a little, well, alien.
Nothing had changed.

But Chris had changed.

He'd seen that the darkness of the universe was
so much bigger and deeper than the darkness in
his room, but he was not afraid. He wanted to
explore every corner of the night sky.

For the first time, Chris could see
the power and mystery and velvety
black beauty of the dark.

And he realised you're never really alone there.
Your dreams are always with you, just waiting.
Big dreams, about the kind of person you want to be.

Wonderful dreams about the life you will live.

Dreams that actually can come true.

ABOUT CHRIS HADFIELD

Growing up, Chris Hadfield spent every summer at his family's cottage on Stag Island in southern Ontario. Like just about everyone else on the island, the Hadfields didn't have a television set, so late in the evening of 20 July 1969, Chris and his family went to a neighbour's cottage to watch the *Apollo 11* landing on TV. When he saw Neil Armstrong step onto the surface of the Moon, Chris's life changed forever. He knew he wanted to be an astronaut too.

At the time, it was impossible. For one thing, he wasn't a grown-up yet. For another, all of NASA's astronauts were American. Canadians weren't even allowed to apply for the job.

But Chris decided to start getting ready, just in case things ever changed. He worked hard at school, learning everything he could about science, rockets and Space. As a teenager, he learned how to fly gliders, and then, after graduating from military college, he became a fighter pilot. Later, he became a test pilot who helped make military aircraft safer. In 1992, almost twenty-three years after that summer night on Stag Island, Chris's dream came true: the newly formed Canadian Space Agency chose him to be an astronaut.

Since then, he has orbited the Earth thousands of times on three separate missions. Most recently, Chris was in Space for nearly five months, from December 2012 to May 2013, when he served as the first Canadian Commander of the International Space Station (ISS).

Today, Chris travels the world teaching people about Space, sharing the beautiful photographs he took and playing the songs he recorded on the space station. On summer nights, he likes to sit on his dock on Stag Island, watching for the ISS to pass by overhead. Even in the darkest dark, on a moonless night, the spaceship's light is clearly visible.

A MESSAGE FROM CHRIS

Being in the dark can feel scary . . . but it's also an amazing place. The dark is where we see the stars and galaxies of our universe. The dark is where we find the Northern Lights shimmering and get to wish on shooting stars. And it was quietly in the dark where I first decided who I was going to be and imagined all the things I could do. The dark is for dreams – and morning is for making them come true.

Chris Hadfield

My first spaceship, 1964.

My family (that's me in the striped shirt), 1966.

Excited to be a glider pilot, 1975.

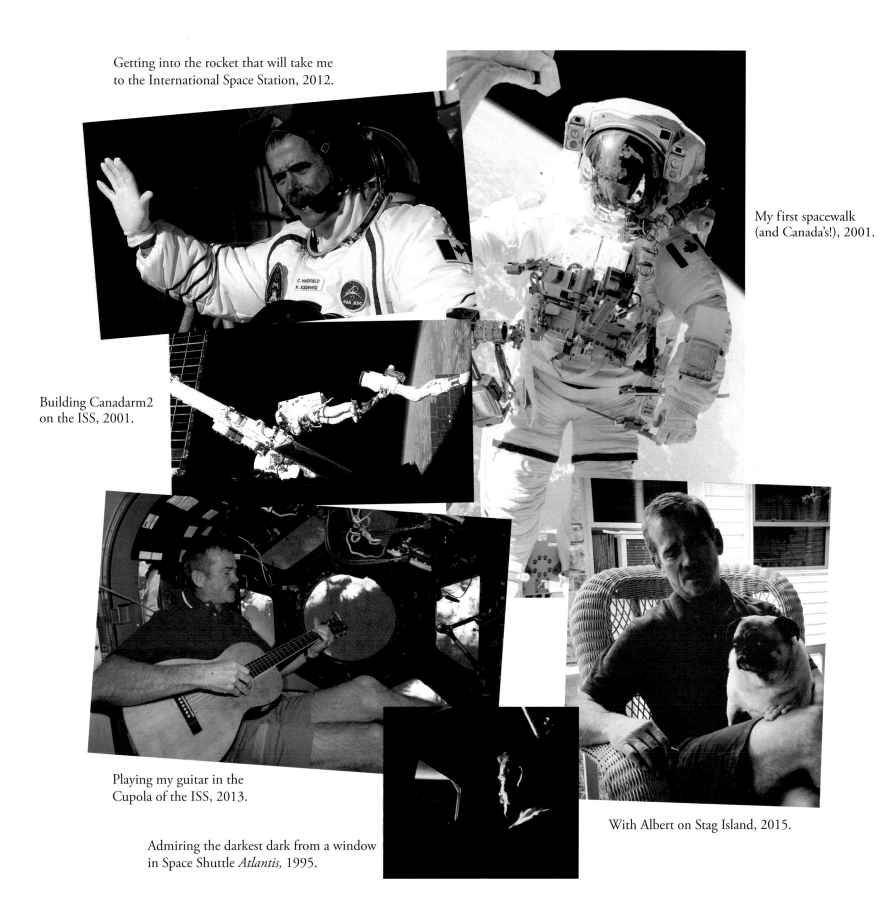

Getting into the rocket that will take me to the International Space Station, 2012.

My first spacewalk (and Canada's!), 2001.

Building Canadarm2 on the ISS, 2001.

Playing my guitar in the Cupola of the ISS, 2013.

Admiring the darkest dark from a window in Space Shuttle *Atlantis,* 1995.

With Albert on Stag Island, 2015.

AUTHOR PHOTOGRAPH: NASA

CHRIS HADFIELD is one of the world's most accomplished astronauts and the international bestselling author of *An Astronaut's Guide to Life on Earth* and *You Are Here: Around the World in 92 Minutes*. Since returning from his third mission, when he served as Commander of the International Space Station and lived in Space for five months, Chris now frequently speaks to audiences throughout the world about Space and encourages children to engage with science. Chris lives in Toronto with his wife, Helene.

KATE FILLION is a bestselling author and journalist who lives in Toronto with her two sons.

TERRY FAN and **ERIC FAN** received their formal art training at the Ontario College of Art and Design. They use ink and graphite mixed with digital art to create magical images of all kinds. The Fans live in Toronto and are the authors and illustrators of *The Night Gardener*, their critically acclaimed debut picture book.